HISTORY OF
ST. AUGUSTINE

**Whimsically Illustrated Account Of
North America's Oldest City**

Jesse W. Love

Narrative, dialogue, and original cartoons created
by Jesse Love.

Illustrations and original cartoon characters created
by Terry Kent.

Cover design and book layout by Sumara Elan Love
www.3wizardz.com

Published by Kaleidoscope Productions
1467 Siskiyou Boulevard, Ste. 9; Ashland, OR 97520
www.kaleidoscope-publications.com

OTHER BOOKS BY JESSE LOVE

HOW TO BUILD A 12'X14' HOOP GREENHOUSE

DEPRESSION FREE! HOLISTIC & MULTIMEDIA SELF-TREATMENT FOR OVERCOMING DEPRESSION WITHOUT DRUGS

HOT SPRINGS OF WESTERN WASHINGTON

11 SIMPLE CHOICES YOU CAN MAKE TO CHANGE THE WORLD

Dedicated to
Lyndi, Tairel, and Kristelle.
I thought of you as I wrote every line.

A special thanks to Ebba.
Your unfailing support and assistance
kept the wheels turning.

A special note of gratitude and appreciation to my wife
Sumara for retyping, scanning and reformatting the
entire book for the second edition.

Introduction

Many people have asked, "Why begin the Whimsically Illustrated History Series with tiny St. Augustine?" This is a particularly important question to publishers, who look at the much larger markets of other historical cities, such as New York and San Francisco.

Those cities along with many others will be given their day in the sun in the future volumes. It was only proper however, that the first book of the new series begin with the first permanent European settlement in the North America.

The United States evolved into an English speaking country, populated chiefly by descendants of immigrants from the British Isles. Because of this, history as generally taught in textbooks has a strong English slant. The contributions of historical personages of other ethnic or national origin are generally missing or very obscure.

Until I visited Florida, I had never heard of St. Augustine. In grade school, I was taught that the Pilgrims at Plymouth Rock and the settlers at Jamestown, Virginia were the founders of North America's first permanent settlements.

Yet, in 1565, Menendez walked ashore with 600 Spanish soldiers and settlers to found San Agustin. Inconveniently for some historians, that was 42 years before the Pilgrims landed at Plymouth Rock, and 55 years before the beginning of the English settlement at Jamestown, Virginia.

I have always loved history; at least the exciting parts about battles, storms, pestilences, etc. Unfortunately, most history books are so slow and plodding, methodically recording every uninteresting detail that I would fall asleep before I ever reached the good parts.

The purpose of the Whimsical History Series is to briefly, but accurately portray historical towns and cities, leaving out all the falling asleep parts, and including only the good stuff. Because we remember things we laugh about the book is completely illustrated, with hopefully humorous cartoons. These are related in a somewhat indirect sort of way to the historical narrative. History purists will probably scorn me, but I didn't write the book for them anyway. I do hope you will find it enjoyable, readable, and enlightening.

Jesse W. Love
St. Augustine, FL
May 1991

The Story Of
St. Augustine

The first inhabitants to the current day St. Augustine and the surrounding St. Johns River were nomadic Native Americans spreading south from northern lands in search of better hunting grounds and more benign climates.

Archaeologically the earliest known village site is

on the St. Johns River in Volusia County, south of St. Augustine. This area was excavated by archaeologists in the late 1880's and dated at 4,000 to 6,000 years old.

These Native Americans are known as the Mt. Taylor Indians, after the area where the first village excavated by archaeologists was located.

Around 4000 B.C. they moved from their inland sites on the St. Johns River to areas along the Atlantic Intracoastal Waterway. This move toward the sea was probably prompted by discovery of a new and easier to obtain food source, such as salt water oysters.

The lifestyle of the Native Americans remained almost unchanged until the coming of the Europeans. Ninety percent of St. Johns County and the land surrounding St. Augustine is swampy. Because of this, village sites on the

habitable ten percent remained for thousands of years. It was used in the same way in perpetuity by countless generations.

Early white settlers reported enormous shell mounds that protruded prominently along the banks of the Intracoastal Waterway. Some extended as high as thirty feet and covered over an acre of ground. Nearby were large sand mounds where the Native Americans buried their dead. Both were mute testimony to the thousands of years that Native villages had occupied the same site.

Upon the arrival of the first Europeans, the Native Americans, then known as Timucuans, were at the zenith of their society. A circular palisade composed of eight foot poles encircled and protected their villages. A typical village contained about twenty houses and one hundred-fifty people. There were numerous villages

along the Intracoastal Waterway and the St. Johns River.

The Timucuans generally built a large circular community house in the center of the village, spacious enough to hold all the villagers and any guests. This building was used for community gatherings, feasts, ceremonies and special occasions. Their thatched roof houses were also built in this same circular fashion.

They grew a variety of vegetables which they, and other Natives, introduced to the Europeans, such as corn, squash, potatoes, and tomatoes. They also used corn cribs to protect the harvest, and preserved their meat and fish on smoking racks.

During the Easter season in the year 1513, Ponce de

Leon left Puerto Rico and followed the Gulf Stream north on a voyage of exploration. He was searching for sources of gold, silver, and the fabled Fountain of Youth.

Ponce landed near current day St. Augustine at the ancient Native American town of Seloy. He called the new land "La Florida," from the old Spanish "Pascua Florida," signifying the season of Easter. He claimed all of North America, its gold, its silver, all its wealth, and its Native American inhabitants, for Spain, and his majesty the King.

During the fifty years following Ponce de Leon's first landing, Spain sent six expeditions to establish settlements in La Florida. Clouds of ravenous mosquitoes

blotted the sun, and feasted on Spanish blood. Demonic wind storms of unbelievable fury destroyed everything they built, and accompanying tidal waves swept all the debris out to sea. Savage natives made unmerciful attacks on the survivors, indignant at the strange interlopers that dared trespass on their lands. All six expeditions failed.

Ponce de Leon returned to La Florida in 1521, with two hundred soldiers. Upon landing they were furiously attacked by natives and driven into the sea. Ponce was gravely injured. They could not remove the arrows protruding from him, and he died in Cuba a few days later.

In the summer of 1564, French adventurers under Rene de Goulaine de Laudonniere, landed at the mouth of the St. Johns River. They succeeded in establishing a fort and colony within raiding distance of the homebound

Spanish treasure galleons. They claimed all the land; natives included, for the French crown, and named the new settlement Ft. Caroline.

The following spring of 1565 the French king sent a fleet from France with supplies and reinforcements. This was a threat that could not go unanswered by Spain. Their preeminence in Europe depended upon a steady flow of gold from the New World, and the safe arrival of the annual Treasure Fleet of the Indies.

That same year King Phillip II of Spain appointed Don Pedro Menendez de Aviles, governor and Adelantado, General of all the kings' forces of La Florida. Furious with the incursion of the French, the king charged Menendez with the settlement of La Florida by Spanish citizens and the armed expulsion of the French and any other foreign nationals.

On June 29th, 1565, Menendez sailed from Cadiz, Spain with ten ships and eleven hundred men. Storms shortly forced their return. However, they departed again

several days later and were met by twenty additional ships coming from the north carrying friends, relatives, priests, farmers and artisans. Altogether over two thousand six hundred men, women and children set sail for La Florida and the New World.

On September 8th, 1565, Don Pedro Menendez de Aviles, Adelantado and first governor of La Florida stepped ashore at the Native American town of Seloy amid much fanfare and pageantry. Banners waved, cannons fired, six hundred soldiers raised their voices in unified cheers. This was an important day for Spain that was to have historical repercussions far into the future.

The large communal house at the center of the village was commandeered to be the first fort until a more suitable one could be built.

Menendez named the town site San Agustin in honor of the Saints day on which he first spied the shores of La Florida. He had his men dig trenches around the village

and strengthen the walls of the communal house as he made immediate plans to rid the land of the heretical French.

On September 18th, 1565, Menendez marched north from San Agustin with five hundred soldiers to attack and capture the French settlement of Fort Caroline. They were caught in the fury of a passing hurricane that brought torrents of rain. Quiet streams swelled into raging rivers as the entire land was flooded. Menendez pressed on through the swampy quagmire toward Fort Caroline; determine to wipe out the French without delay, hurricanes notwithstanding. Most of his men however,

had never been in such a storm, and nearly one hundred of them took refuge along the route, unable to push on through the storm, and never arriving at Ft. Caroline.

At dawn on September 20th, the remaining Spanish

army attacked the fort. The French were caught completely unprepared. They had few sentries on duty, feeling the hurricane precluded any danger of attack. One hundred thirty-two French soldiers were killed, while Menendez spared the one hundred and eight women and children. The Spaniards lost almost no soldiers in the attack. The victory was well earned, and the march through the swamps during a hurricane would be remembered for generations.

Shortly upon his return to San Agustin from his victory over Fort Caroline, Menendez learned from Native Americans of a large group of white men working their way north along the coast. Suspecting these to be

French soldiers whose vessels had sunk in the hurricane, he gathered a force of fifty men and hurried south to intercept them. From their camp that night on the south end of Anastasia Island they could see the campfires across the inlet of the French.

On the next morning, September 29th, Menendez met a French delegation that was ferried across in a supply boat. Upon learning of the defeat of Fort Caroline the weary, hungry Frenchmen, who were indeed survivors of the hurricane that destroyed their ships, surrendered to Menendez. Once the two hundred men had been fed and bound, Menendez ordered them put to the sword, much to their helpless consternation.

On October 12th, this macabre scene was repeated at the same inlet when Menendez met another group of castaways led by the Admiral of the Fleet, Jean Ribault.

Some members of his party escaped by fleeing south

in the night, rather than trust their lives to the dubious mercies of Menendez. The remainder offered one hundred thousand ducats for their lives, which Menendez declined. As the group that had proceeded them, they surrendered, were given a last meal, bound, then put to the sword.

Altogether, over 250 Frenchmen were slain at the inlet that became known as "Matanzas," or "place of slaughters." Only the musicians and fourteen people who claimed to be Catholic were spared.

The defeat of Fort Caroline, the hurricane's destruction of the French fleet, and the execution of the 350 castaways, permanently ended the threat of French rivalry in east Florida. In just two short months Menendez had succeeded in securing La Florida for Spain.

In 1586, the English privateer Sir Francis Drake, with forty-two vessels and two thousand men stopped by San Agustin en route to England after his successful sack of Cartagena, Columbia.

The Spanish had erected an unlit watchtower near the ocean beach to give early warning of approaching enemy ships. Had Drake not seen this tower he would have passed by San Agustin, as he was unsure of its exact location.

Faced with huge English armada standing off the coast, the Spanish buried their artillery in the sand and all the people withdrew to the woods. In the confusion of their hasty retreat, they forgot to take the royal coffer containing the payroll.

Preceded by Native American looters, Drake's men completed the sack of San Agustin. They cut down the orange trees, uprooted the gardens, and set all the

houses and the wooden fort to the torch. The returning townspeople found only ashes remaining of what they had spent twenty years building.

The year 1599 was a very bad one for San Agustin. The first great fire of its history gutted the Franciscan Friary and destroyed many adjacent areas of town.

Months of hard labor succeeded in rebuilding most of the dwellings and shops that had been lost. However, in early October, a devastating hurricane struck the town, accompanied by an enormous tidal surge. Many of the houses and buildings were carried away by the rising sea. A Native American village, and the island it was located on in the middle of the harbor, was totally submerged by the ocean water. The entire village and all the inhabitants

were lost. The island in the middle of the harbor never reappeared.

The Native Americans and the Europeans loved to trade. According to medical historians, among the first things the Europeans gave the natives were smallpox, measles, typhoid, and cholera. The Native Americans, in turn, gave syphilis to the white man to take back to Europe.

The Spaniard at first did not fear syphilis. It caused only some sores and inconvenient itching. However, syphilis is an insidious disease. It sometimes takes over

twenty years for it to develop into its third and most deadly stage. Within the next hundred years it spread like wildfire across the countries of Europe, killing over ten million people.

Back in La Florida, Bubonic plague was carried ashore in 1613 by rats from visiting ships. It spread quickly through the native population. Spanish Friars estimated that over twenty-five thousand Native Americans died throughout La Florida in the next four years.

In 1638 King Philip IV of Spain was in desperate financial straits because of the drain from Spain's involvement in the Thirty Year War in Europe. To help pay the creditors he ordered the return to the treasury of all monies earmarked for the overseas colonies. This caused immediate and catastrophic consequences throughout

the New World. For the thirty years there was almost no cash money in circulation. Nearly all transactions were by barter or promissory notes.

As citizens of San Agustin were digesting the glum news that there would be no supply ship from Spain that year, they were hit by the worst hurricane in forty years. Much of the town was severely damaged, and rebuilding was slowed by lack of coin to pay the workers.

In 1649 the annual Treasure Fleet of the Indies that left Vera Cruz, Mexico in the spring, had Yellow Fever infected mosquito larvae in its water casks. At its next stop, Havana, Cuba the epidemic killed one third of the population and quickly spread north with the mosquitoes.

At San Agustin, nearly one half of the population died. The social, religious, military, and economic order, were all shattered. For among the dead were all the Friars; the governor of La Florida; the commanding officer of the fort and military garrison; the two Captains of Companies, who were the next most superior officers; and the two officials of the King's Treasury, who were the only people authorized to dispense money or payroll from the royal coffers.

This was followed seven years later by a measles epidemic. The Europeans had built up some immunity, through generations of exposure to this disease. The natives however, had no defense, and over ten thousand died that year throughout La Florida.

In 1668, the English privateer Robert Searls, executed an ingenious and successful plan for the capture of the

fort at San Agustin. He waited offshore for several days beyond the sight of coastal lookouts. Finally he spotted a ship that had just departed San Agustin. He quickly engaged and captured it. A prize crew including Captain Searls and most of his buccaneers, then turned the captured ship back toward the harbor of San Agustin.

The coastal lookout seeing the Spanish ship returning gave no alarm. In fact, the harbor pilot came out to guide the ship across the channel bar and into safe anchorage. The buccaneers, dressed in Spanish uniforms, captured the unsuspecting harbor pilot and his boat. They used it to ferry the entire crew to shore in the darkness of night.

The sentries at the fort were likewise fooled by the charade, and Captain Searls and his men were within the walls before anyone saw through their masquerade.

The fort quickly fell to the bloodthirsty pirates. Once it was neutralized, the pirates rampaged through the town. Sixty people were killed. Everyone not of pure Spanish blood was rounded up to be sold into slavery. Personal jewelry and family heirlooms were wrenched from the hands of the terrified townspeople. One hundred thirty-eight marks of silver were taken from the royal treasury, leaving the colony no money to pay for essential supplies.

In order to not discourage the townspeople too much, that he might return to raid another day, Captain Searls did not burn the town.

After years of petitioning the king, monies to construct a stone fortress were finally allotted from Spain to San Agustin. Royal Engineers arrived shortly thereafter and began planning the construction.

In 1672, massive bocks of coquina stone quarried on Anastasia Island were laid for the foundation of Castillo

San Marcos. Coquina is a unique stone that proved to be providential in being used to construct the Castillo. It is soft when quarried, but quickly hardens in the sun.

The Castillo employed the most advanced designs

ever achieved in fort construction. From its geometrically constructed ramparts would-be attackers were exposed to withering cross fire from any point of attack. Its seventy-seven cannons commanded a 360 degree field of fire. The largest fired a twenty-four pound cannonball up to three miles beyond the fort. Once the enormous coquina stone walls were in place and mounted with cannons, pirates and privateers never bothered San Agustin again.

Countries around the world have long claimed a territorial right to the sea up to three miles from the shore. This originated in the days of the Castillo, and is based upon the maximum firing distance of shore-based cannons—three miles.

By way of comparison, the largest cannons of a World War II US. Navy, Iowa Class Battleship can hurl a two thousand pound shell up to twenty-five miles.

The next several decades were punctuated by intense

25

28

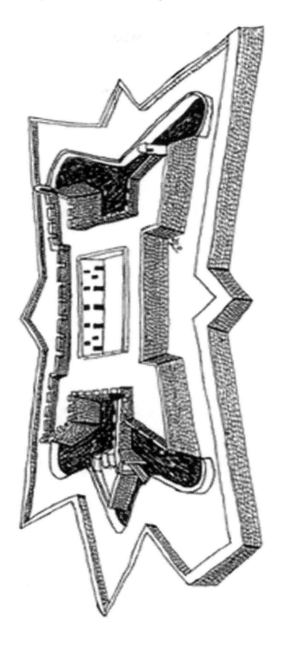

Castillo de San Marco

rivalry between the Spanish and English crowns. And one of their favorite battlegrounds was the New World colonies.

England had established substantial settlements in Georgia and South Caroline. Spain's bastion in North America was San Agustin. The English had decided that if they could capture San Agustin, Spain would be driven off the continent.

In 1702, Governor James Moore, of South Carolina, led a land and naval assault on the Castillo.

Governor Zuniga, of San Agustin, saw there was no safe way to defend the town. He ordered all twelve hundred townspeople and three hundred soldiers into the Castillo for protection. Zuniga sent out troops to destroy homes near the Castillo to prevent their use as cover to the enemy.

Governor Moore's troops encircled the fort and began a siege that was to last eight long hot weeks but prove fruitless.

The thick coquina walls of the fortress were unlike any other ever encountered. Because of the stones soft porous composition, cannonballs had little effect. The walls absorbed the tremendous impacts with little or no damage.

When Spanish warships were spotted offshore Moore panicked. Afraid that if they tried to escape on their ships they would be captured, he ordered them burned in the harbor. The army then marched overland in an inglorious retreat to Georgia.

The ships had been privately owned and pressed into service by Moore. Their owners were furious that he had burned them, and Moore was haunted by his defeat till

the end of his days.

In 1712 English privateers captured the annual supply and treasury ship en route to San Agustin from Spain. Famine hit the town which was still far from self-dependent, and relied heavily on foods and stores brought in by ships from Spain and the Caribbean colonies. Before another supply ship made it through to San Agustin, most of the cats, dogs, and horses had disappeared. They were consumed to feed a famished people.

The English were determined to capture San Agustin. In June 1740, British General James Oglethorpe began a land and naval siege of the Castillo. The Spanish however, were able to get food and provisions through from Cuba. And as in Governor Moore's previous siege—four weeks of constant bombardment had little effect on the unique coquina walls of the Castillo.

By the end of July, his naval forces were insistent upon leaving before the advent of the worst months of the hurricane season. It had been a very dry, hot summer, and his soldiers were near mutiny. They baked in the day, and were harassed to desperation at night by hordes of hungry mosquitoes. The fact that even their largest, most powerful cannonballs could not breach the walls of the Castillo did not help their morale. Under these circumstances Oglethorpe reluctantly withdrew his forces to Georgia.

The English had succeeded in capturing the annual

supply and treasury ship from Spain three consecutive years—1739, 1740 and 1741. San Agustin was desperate for food. Under these trying circumstances the Governor commissioned privateers to attack and capture enemy vessels. The results were excellent, and greatly lifted the spirits of the townspeople.

The first capture was a ship out of Charleston with a load of rice. In a letter to the Governor of Cuba, Governor Montiano of San Agustin said, "It has been the salvation of this city, because from the 28th of October when she came in, the troops and entire town have lived on it."

By Christmas 1741, there were thirteen captured English vessels at anchor by the Castillo. Their cargos had provided Madera wine, beans, pork, the staples of corn and flour, and some luxury items.

Following the Seven Years War with England, the Spanish crown reluctantly ceded San Agustin and all of

east Florida to the English, at the Treaty of Paris in 1763.

As part of the settlement, the English returned Havana, Cuba, which they had captured, to Spain. Thus, Spain retained one of the central cities of their colonial empire, while only giving up an important, but remote, settlement.

The Spanish citizens of San Agustin feared reprisals from the British. They began a rapid mass exodus for Havana, Cuba and Vera Cruz, Mexico. Just one year later, the church counted only eight Catholics in all of Florida.

To encourage colonization, the English King granted vast tracts of land to wealthy Englishmen. He deeded one hundred thousand acres, seventy miles south of St.

Augustine, to Andrew Turnbull; a Scottish physician of London. In return, Turnbull agreed to bring in colonists and clear the land.

Shortly thereafter, Turnbull brought over fifteen hundred immigrants to Florida as indentured servants. Most of these were of Greek, Italian, and Minorcan origin.

Turnbull however, was a cruel taskmaster, and declined to free any of his laborers from their indenture. In 1768 as many as fifteen people a day were dying from the deplorable living and working conditions he forced upon them.

In March of 1777, multiple delegations of laborers

journeyed to St. Augustine to plead their case to the English governor, Patrick Tonyn. The governor was outraged at their plight and issued orders resulting in the release from indenture of all of Turnbull's laborers.

During the American Revolutionary War, St. Augustine was staunchly royalist. The Castillo had been renamed Castle St. Mark, and the military garrison there actively participated in prosecuting the war against the rebellious colonies.

Frequent raids were conducted north across the Georgia border to capture salves and cattle. In February 1777, East Florida Rangers captured and burned Ft. McIntosh in Georgia, and returned to St. Augustine with two thousand head of cattle. Similar raids were conducted by the American into English East Florida.

In March of 1778, East Florida Rangers captured and burned Ft. Barrington on the Altamaha River in Georgia. The Americans counterattacked with a force of three thousand men. They captured Ft. Tonyn and moved

south down the St. Johns River. East Florida Rangers met them in a fierce battle at the Alligator River Bridge on the Nassau River, and turned the Americans back into Georgia.

In the summer of 1778, over two thousand reinforcements poured into St. Augustine to join in an attack on forts and settlements in Georgia. This force marched all the way to Savannah, leaving a path of destruction in their wake.

On October 19th, 1781, British General Cornwallis surrendered his seven thousand troops to American General George Washington., at Yorktown, Virginia. Panic stricken and disbelieving royalists from South Carolina and Georgia fled to St. Augustine for refuge.

All had the hope that the British crown would retain this vital fortified city, and keep it a safe haven for royalists.

Dozens of ships came each month, bringing not only the fleeing loyalists, but all their personal property, slaves, munitions and military stores, as well as all the loyalist troops from South Carolina and Georgia. At least sixteen ships carrying refuges went aground trying to clear the treacherous channel bar into St. Augustine's harbor.

Spanish power had been rebuilding throughout the Caribbean during the American Revolutionary War. They had retained West Florida, and in the 1783 Treaty of Paris, which formally ended the Revolutionary War, the English ceded East Florida back to the Spanish.

In July of 1784 Governor Zespedes of Spain, came ashore with five hundred troops to take command of Castle St. Mark, which was quickly given its old name of Castillo San Marcos.

The following year saw a transitional government, shared by Governor Zespedes and ex-Governor Tonyn.

By 1786 over one half of the English citizens of San Agustin had departed rather than profess Catholicism as required by the Spanish Governor. All the loyalists that had escaped to St. Augustine after the war now began an exodus to the Bahamas, which was the last bastion of British sovereignty in the area. Many left prosperous plantation behind, but chose loss of their lands rather than being subject to rule under either Americans in Georgia and South Carolina, or Spaniards in Florida.

Neither England nor Spain, long time Emperors of the New World had reckoned with the relentless "manifest destiny" of the Americans. Thirty-six years after the English gave up all their colonies to the Americans, the

Spanish likewise capitulated.

In the Adams-Onis treaty of 1819, Spain transferred all of Florida to the United States. A formal ceremony and transfer of flags took place at the Castillo on July 10, 1821.

Spain was paid for Florida, and that fact was hotly contested in the United States Congress before the purchase. John Randolph, a representative of the U.S. House, had this to say concerning the proposed acquisition of Florida—"Florida, sire, is not worth buying. It is a land of swamps, of quagmires, of frogs, and alligators, and mosquitoes! A man, sir, would not immigrate to Florida. No sir! No, not even from Hell itself!"

Settlers did come to Florida though, despite Randolph's prediction. But many soon wondered if he hadn't been right. In 1821, a Yellow Fever epidemic wiped out a good portion of the town's population. Thomas Fitch, the newly appointed judge, his wife, and all his children, were among the first victims.

As more northern whites began moving in the Florida territory, the Seminole Native Americans were pushed off the best land, and further into the swamps by the land hungry settlers. Tensions and skirmishes began rising all along the frontier as the Seminoles began asserting that they would be pushed no further.

The Seminoles themselves were recent immigrants. They had migrated to Florida less than one hundred years earlier. They filled the void left by the vanished Timucuan Native Americans, whom had been completely exterminated by a combination of foreign diseases and

decimating attacks by Europeans of all persuasions—French, Spanish, and English. By 1719, a Spaniard walking from St. Augustine to the Chattahoochee River in the west reported not a single sign of Native Americans in all the land.

During the period of 1835-1841, three costly wars were waged in Florida against the fierce Seminoles. By 1839, most of the action had shifted to the Everglades, but prior to that St, Augustine was a hotspot.

In October 1836, under the guise of a flag of truce, two hundred-fifty troops of the U.S. Army captured Osceola, one of the most famous chiefs of the Seminoles, and seventy-five of his warriors and sub-chiefs near St. Augustine. They were imprisoned inside the Castillo, but six weeks later the sub-chiefs and nineteen warriors escaped. Osceola was then shipped north to Ft. Moultrie in Charleston, South Carolina where he died shortly thereafter. The remaining Seminoles at the Castillo were shipped west to Oklahoma Native American Territory.

Strong leaders continued to emerge from within the Seminole tribe, and during the next five years, they waged one of the most successful wars against the U.S. Army of any of the Native American nations.

During the year 1845, Florida became the 27th state of the United States. As a compromise between Pensacola in the far west, and St. Augustine in the far east, Tallahassee was selected as the capital. It was situated about half way between these two regional centers.

For the next decade St. Augustine prospered as wealthy people from the north began coming to the city to vacation and settle.

This peaceful reverie was broken by the outbreak

of the Civil War in 1861. It divided the city, which had strong Union sentiments, due to its large population of northerners, and relatively minor use of slaves in its non-agrarian economy.

When the state of Florida seceded from the union, most of St. Augustine's northern born citizens left to return to northern states.

The Castillo San Marcos was taken possession of by Confederate troops from the state of Florida, and most of the cannons were removed and carried north to defend Jacksonville. Despite the Castillo, St. Augustine was considered an insignificant town, and only small garrisons of Confederate troops were posted at the fort.

In March 1862, when a Union blockade squadron appeared in the harbor, the few Confederate soldiers slipped away at night. The next morning the Union troops accepted the cities surrender and occupied the

Castillo for the duration of the war.

Between 1875-1886, the government shipped trouble-making Native Americans from the western states to be imprisoned in the Castillo, far away from where they could harm incoming white settlers. Members of Geronimo's band were among those interned. This is an interesting twist to the government's policy just thirty years earlier, when the Seminole of Florida were shipped west to Oklahoma.

The army officer in charge of the Castillo was Captain Richard Pratt. He gave the Native Americans much freedom within the Castillo. Pratt believed that the natives, as a race, could only survive if they stopped being curious stone-age oddities. To facilitate this he had them cut their hair, dressed them in full army uniforms, drilled them in army marching, and began an education process for them.

Due to the success of his efforts, a Native American School was started in Pennsylvania. A few years later, when the natives were given the choice of going to the new Native American School or returning to the reservations in the west, many elected to remain in the east and attend the school.

St. Augustine had always been an isolated town. Its chief purpose for hundreds of years had been as a garrison for the military. The Spanish had originally chosen the town site to act as a buffer in the northern part of their territories. They build the Castillo both to protect the town, and prevent the southern expansion of the English.

The hazardous sand bar across the harbor channel prevented St. Augustine's use as a major trading port or naval base. Large vessels could not enter the harbor.

For most of its history, the town had little or no economic base. The minimal farming done in the area was insufficient to even feed the local population.

When Tallahassee became the state capital, Jacksonville the major port and population center in the area, and the Castillo no longer an active military garrison, St. Augustine was on the verge of becoming a forgotten, sleepy, backwater hamlet. It was accessible only to the wealthy who could afford the time and money to reach it. It required long journey by boat down the St. Johns River, followed by an eighteen mile carriage trip from Palatka on obscure dirt roads.

Then two events happened that were destined to revive St. Augustine, and lead to it becoming the popular tourist attraction it is today.

The first was the completion in 1883, of the St.

Augustine & Halifax River Railway, which connected south Jacksonville to St. Augustine. This made trips to the historic town possible for average people, and ended St. Augustine's isolation.

The second was the interest the visionary Henry M. Flagler took in St. Augustine. In a matter of a few years he transformed the town. He purchased the newly completed railroad line, and eventually ran the tracks all the way to Key West. Flagler saw the potential of St. Augustine

as a tourist Mecca, with its white sand beaches, historic Castillo, and sunny climate.

As owner of the Standard Oil Company, and one of the richest men in the world, Flagler poured money into St. Augustine to fulfill his dream.

Whenever Flagler set himself to a project it was with the intent to make it grander, and do it better, than it would be possible for anyone else to do or duplicate. Today, the Hotel Ponce de Leon, now Flagler College, stands as an architecturally stunning monument in St. Augustine, to the visions and drive of Henry M. Flagler. In 1893 an article in Vogue Magazine

Said of the Pone—"It is as if some modern Haroun-Al-Raschid deserted his own palace and turned it into a hotel."

True to his belief, tens of thousands of tourists of all economic classes, and from around the world, came to St. Augustine. They came riding his train, to stay in his hotels.

Within a few years Flagler's attention shifted south. He ran his railroad down the east coast of Florida and jump started many other communities even as he had St. Augustine.

Though Flagler departed to fulfill still greater dreams, the architecturally magnificent buildings he created remained; another page in St. Augustine's history and a monument to Flagler, even as the Castillo is a monument to the glory of what once was Imperial Spain.

By the 1880's people from the northern states had returned to St. Augustine in droves, both to live and vacation. Many new hotels were built to accommodate the tourists. On April 27yh, 1887, the four story St.

Augustine Hotel caught fire. The blaze quickly spread through the area north of the plaza. It eventually consumed many homes and businesses, as well as the Old Catholic Cathedral.

In 1888, a Yellow Ever scare caused many of the town's white inhabitants to flee north. This unusual circumstance gave the black citizens a temporary voting majority, which produced at least on city councilman and a few black police officers during the new few years.

The Yellow Fever epidemic was largely confined to southern Florida. To insure that remained the case, city officials quarantined and cordoned off the entire town. Any outsiders attempting to enter were turned back by shotgun; mail service was discontinued because of fear of "contamination by microbes."

Even at this late date in the century, it was still believed by medical professionals that Yellow Fever was a communicable disease. It was not yet known that it was carried by the mosquitoes which crossed the cordon line, and beat the quarantine with ease.

In 1894, a major hurricane swept with fury into St. Augustine. Most of the wooden buildings in town were left piles of debris. The local fishing fleet was deposited high and dry, and blocks away from the receding sea.

The winter of that same year, the "worst freeze in memory," swept through the entire state. In St. Augustine water pipes at the Hotel Ponce de Leon burst. Local oranges froze as solid as rocks on the trees, and all the tropical foliage blackened and died.

On April 2, 1914, a fire broke out at the Florida House Hotel and spread throughout the old city. Fire departments from as far away as Jacksonville came to help fight the fire. Nevertheless, five blocks of hotels, businesses and historic landmarks were left smoldering

ruins.

This was St. Augustine's last major catastrophe, as modern methods of building, fire fighting, and health care began winning the battles against the scourges that had plagued St. Augustine for over four hundred years.

After the fire of 1914, St. Augustine graduated into 20th century contemporary American life. Its history from that point resembles many other small towns across the country. But the 400 years that preceded that—ah, that was something very unique in America.

So the next time you're in one of those dry old history classes, and your instructor tell you that the first settlements in North America were at Plymouth rock and Jamestown, don't let it pass. Take a moment to tell your instructor the wonderful story of St. Augustine... and from Jesse and Terry, thank you for letting us tell the story to you.

BIBLIOGRAPHY AND SUGGESTED ADDITIONAL READING

1. Guide to Florida lighthouses, by Elinor De Wire. Published by Pineapple Press Inc. 1987.

2. Spanish St. Augustine; The Archeology of a Colonial Creole Community, by Kathleen Deegan. Published by Academic Press 1983.

3. Stories of Old St. Augustine, by Virginia Edward. Published by Paramount Press 1973.

4. Florida's Menendez; Captain General of the Ocean Sea, by Albert Manucy. Published by St. Augustine Historical Society 1965.

5. Before the White Man: Pre-history of St. Johns County, Florida, by James M. Smith. Published by Historic St. Augustine Preservation Board 1975.

6. The Oldest City: St. Augustine, Saga of Survival, by (eight different authors). Published by St. Augustine Historic Society 1983.

7. The Cathedral-Basilica of St. Augustine and its

History, Author unknown. Publisher unknown.

ABOUT THE AUTHOR

I have been blessed with some amazing experiences in my life that certainly have influenced me to have a desire to help the people of the world. Many of my books penned under both Jesse Love and Embrosewyn Tazkuvel are written with that goal in mind. I've been fortunate to have traveled to many countries around the world and interacted with people from the president of the country to the family living in a shack with a dirt floor. Being among people of many cultures, religions and social standings, watching them in their daily lives, seeing their hopes and aspirations for their children and the joys they have with their families and friends, has continually struck me with a deep feeling of oneness. I've been with elderly people as they breathed their last breath and at the birth of babies when they take their first. It's all very humbling. This amazing world we live in and the wonderful people that fill it have given me so much. My books are my way to give back as much as I can to as many people as I can.

You can contact me through the Contact Us form on www.celestopea.com.

If you have enjoyed this book, I would be honored if you would take a few moments to visit the book page on Amazon and leave a review for the book. JESSE'S BOOKS

Jesse and Terry

Jesse's Books

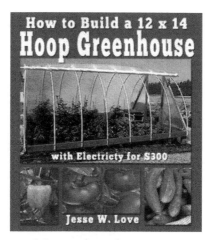

How to Build a 12'x14' Hoop Greenhouse with Electricity for $300

Grow your own organic vegetables and enjoy fresh flowers late into the winter and early in the spring with your sturdy, homemade hoop greenhouse. An easy to follow, step-by-step guide to building a spacious 12'x14' greenhouse using steel reinforced PVC pipe that stands up to high winds and heavy snows! Includes bonus plans to add electricity for winter heating. One person, even with little or no building experience, can build it in a weekend with the easy to follow step-by-step plans that include detailed drawings, 25 closeup pictures, and a complete list with pictures of every component, fastener and tool you will need to make it perfect.

Hot Springs of Western Washington

Over 250 hot springs and soda pop springs are detailed in this classic book. Filled with enticing pictures, easy to follow maps, GPS coordinates, historical information and current status, this book is a must have for any hot spring enthusiast. Whether you are looking to find privacy in a remote wilderness spring or be pampered in a five star resort, Hot Springs of Western Washington will help you find the way to your hot spring bliss.

In addition to the heavenly hot springs, this is still the only book available that guides you to the location of the natural soda pop springs in Washington. Bottle your own naturally carbonated water as it bubbles out of the mountains. Add some flavoring of your choice when you get home and you have pioneer soda pop! Or, chill it in the fridge overnight and enjoy delicious sparkling water the next day.

Customers Who Bought This Item Also Bought

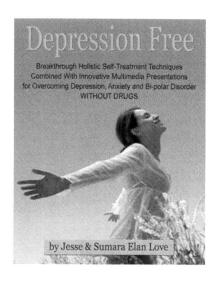

Depression Free

Breakthrough Holistic Self-Treatment Techniques
Combined With Innovative Multimedia Presentations
for Overcoming Depression, Anxiety and Bi-polar Disorder
WITHOUT DRUGS

by Jesse & Sumara Elan Love

DEPRESSION FREE
Holistic & Multimedia Self-treatment for
Overcoming Depression WITHOUT DRUGS

Depression Free presents a revolutionary holistic approach to self-treating depression, anxiety and Bi-polar Disorder, naturally, without drugs.

Startling breakthrough techniques including Brainswitching, the Lanaka, and Sun Gazing are presented in detail so you can begin immediate and effective self-treatment.

The heart of Depression Free is an innovative multi-media program that combines harmonious music, rythmic sound, beautiful supporting images, and short positive affirmations flashing on your computer or TV, to beneficially affect your brain chemical balance and bring your mood and entire body into a calm, peaceful and upbeat state.

You will be amazed at the immediate affect of just a single 10 minute session and the lasting, dramatic, personal transformation as you continue to view the positive, hypnotic affirmations 3-4 times a day from your choice of the 14 presented in Depression Free. Banish your demons and say hello to a new you of happiness, smiles and positive attitudes. A new you that has greater success in life, career and relationships without the burden of the dark demons you were carrying inside your heart and mind.

Everyone can benefit from the positive, hypnotic affirmations and the other 9 holistic techniques presented in Depression Free; not just people suffering from depression. If you've ever wanted to banish your demons, have better health, happy more fulfilling relationships, greater success and simply unleash your greatest potential, this is the book for you!

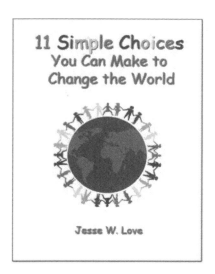

11 SIMPLE CHOICES YOU CAN MAKE TO CHANGE THE WORLD

Entertaining and enlightening, this book shares the secret of changing the world by making 11 simple life choices. Each choice is presented with multiple specific ways to implement the choice. Many interesting stories are interwoven sharing real-life experiences and successes. A must read for anyone who truly wishes to make a difference in the world today and leave a wonderful legacy for generations to come.

Made in the USA
Middletown, DE
12 November 2019